Song of Paper

what is this song of paper
singing itself to itself?

… often there is no 'I' writing the poem, but rather an instrument playing a
larger song that belongs to us all. ~ Cynthia Jobin

Song of Paper

Cynthia Jobin

Bennison Books
A good book is a blessing

Bennison Books Poetic Licence
978-1-9997408-1-8

bennisonbooks.com

Contents

Introduction

At the end of November 2016, I received a startling email from Cynthia Jobin. Cynthia lived in New England, I in old England, and we had become acquainted through the Internet and our love of poetry. We gave each other encouragement and supportive criticism and I was delighted when in 2014 she sent me a copy of *A Certain Age*, a privately published hardback edition of her poems. Otherwise, Cynthia's work was largely unpublished in her lifetime except via her blog, but there she gained a loyal international readership; devotees appreciated her keen intellect and abundant humanity.

That November email was short and to the point: she had been diagnosed with terminal cancer and wanted a few of her Internet friends to know. She closed by saying simply "A new journey begun ...".

In trying to reply adequately, I encouraged her to think about the legacy of her poetry, to find someone to take care of her blog, her book, and poems yet to come. She responded by saying that she was puzzling about what to do with the large number of poems which she had intended to include in a second collection.

I wrote back with a suggestion from my wife: that we could approach my own publisher, Bennison Books, here in Britain and I offered to help in any way I could. Cynthia replied immediately to agree to this proposal but died before sending me her poems. I learnt of her death only indirectly through a brief announcement made on her blog.

An international collaboration

Thankfully, that was not the end of the story. A year later, an old friend of Cynthia's, Julie Murray, set out on a quest to contact Cynthia's heirs and find a way to bring the poems back to their readers. Cynthia's sister, Jennifer, came into the story next – emerging from a long period of grief and wondering what could be done to preserve the poetry. Meanwhile, in New Zealand, Bruce Goodman stepped forward: a steadfast Internet friend of Cynthia's, he had kept all the poems that had appeared on her blog. And here in Britain, Deborah Bennison agreed that I would compile the book and her independent publishing house would take on the role of pro bono editor and publisher. Together we became a sort of project team, and this book is the happy result.

Cynthia Jobin's poetry is skilfully crafted and both erudite and accessible. She wrote about the mysteries of life, her grief following the death of her partner of 43 years, love and friendship, the joy of pets and the landscape of New England. She also translated French poetry. There was a depth of feeling and an unobtrusive intellect at work, but equally a lightness of touch and humour. The poems in this collection show that variety of theme and equally her range of tone; she would write just for fun as well as with serious intent.

These lines from *Patient Belongings* illustrate the clarity of her writing:

> *Your earrings and I,*
> *with only the turned-off machines*
> *pushed back against the walls to overhear*
>
> *said our appalling last goodbye. Then*

> *stunned to a disbelief way beyond sorrow,*
> *we went home. In time*
>
> *I gave the earrings to your sister –*
> *as you know, she is a fool for jewelry –*
> *and felt they should be hers.*

Other poems however are upbeat in tone. For example, in *A Dog in the Grass* we find her characteristic blend of thought, observation and warmth:

> *That being said, the trick is*
> *to stand camera-less*
> *within a spot of sun*
> *just looking, listening, and*
> *smell the lilac, taste the timothy*
>
> *as moment fades*
> *into another moment – stay*
> *and watch the dog get up,*
> *shake her whole skin, raise*
> *snout to sniff, then trot away.*

Moving tributes

Cynthia and her partner were recently retired teachers (one in mathematics and one in the arts). They had just bought a home in New Hampshire, midway between the mountains and the sea, were in good health and looking forward to many new good things. But in August 2010, a cerebral haemorrhage ended her partner's life. Cynthia then developed a cancerous tumour which she attributed directly to that loss – the connection of mind and body patently obvious. But while her poetry spoke of grief, love, happy memories and the trials of aging, she kept her illness to herself for a long time.

It is unsurprising that Cynthia had so many longstanding blog followers and Internet friends. As the news of her death rippled out, many fine tributes were posted online. One of the first was the single word 'Heartbroken' and many paid moving tributes to the person they felt had come to be a friend. Other tributes included appreciations of her poetry. The UK writer Paul Beech, articulating the thoughts of so many, wrote:

> *With her wide vocabulary and mastery of form, her humanity, humour and skill in painting pictures in the mind, Cynthia was a most amazing and versatile poet. Her finely-wrought work was not only entertaining but deeply moving and thought-provoking too, playful and profound by turns, even sometimes inviting contemplation of the great mysteries.*

Mastery of form

He was right to mention her mastery of form. Although Cynthia often wrote in free verse, unrhymed and contemporary, she was fascinated by traditional forms. I believe her intellect relished the challenge of working within their constraints: not just filling up the lines with the right number of words and syllables, but discovering the hidden operations of those forms to give her lines extra power. And yet, as her poetry and the conversation on her blog revealed, she had a playful sense of humour; she set more than a handful of poets racing to rival her, for example, when she burst into song with a traditional Irish droighneach.

When reading a new poem from Cynthia Jobin I have always had that comfortable feeling of being in good hands: we know that the verses are going to be impeccably crafted but we can't predict what path they will take.

I am sure that new readers and old friends alike will discover this for themselves on reading this collection. The title, *Song of Paper*, comes from the opening poem and feels so apposite. The closing poem, which was also the last she ever posted in life, and which shows humour even in the midst of wisdom and courage, is an immensely moving reflection from someone who knew herself to be very close to death.

John Looker, 2018

John Looker is the author of *The Human Hive* published by Bennison Books. His work has also been published internationally in a number of journals and anthologies.

About the Author

The New England poet Cynthia Jobin died in late 2016. Her poetry was admired and enjoyed internationally by the many followers of her blog and readers of *A Certain Age*, a collection of her work published privately in a limited edition. Her work was also featured in the anthology *Indra's Net* (Bennison Books, 2017) and had been published in a number of journals. Her writing richly deserves even wider attention.

Immediately after graduating, Cynthia taught in private and public schools. As she explained: 'After seven years, I left that work because I wanted to "be a writer" (*Cynthia's quotation marks*) … In those years I did many odd jobs, worked in community theatre and learned the traditional craft of calligraphy …'

The post from which she finally retired was adjunct professor of graduate students, lecturing in history, aesthetics and research at the Massachusetts College of Art and Design. She always considered poetry her vocation.

'And now, that's what I do,' she said after retiring. 'I read and write poems.'

Cynthia was also a warm and generous supporter of other writers.

Part One

Love Knows Not

Awake, My Soul

Sniff the bitter grass
teaser on a passing breeze.
Shall we plant sweet peas?

Snow lies still in the garden.
Clouds hang heavy from heaven.

Stiffened hands and feet
yearn to cut loose from their wraps
to wriggle in sun.

See how the day lasts longer.
Chickadee, where have you been?

The sun has spoken.
Shadows caress the mountain.
I call out to them

we wait for the lulling of
night crickets rubbing their wings.

Feather in my hand
crisp leaf that skitters windborne
nowhere in my head

what is this song of paper
singing itself to itself?

Now it is April
the frail old stoop-sitter smiles
but he says nothing.

Still Life With Prickly Pears

Two prickly pears in a small bowl
of old majolica posed on a silken stole
ask will you be my valentine…
recall a sweet Venetian barcarole.

Cactus creatures pocked with tiny spines
they stab the skin like quills of porcupine;
they do not kill but finely cut the wounds
of will you be my valentine…

Deep red the foreground drapery is strewn
with fruit skins and a plate of macaroons
heart-shaped, in bastard amber light –
eternity is where it's always afternoon.

The atmosphere floods with gemütlichkeit;
a goblet filled and ready to be raised invites
once more, then, will you be my valentine…?
The background says: I think I might.

Notes for a Sonnet

I fall in love with
what cannot be mine

a lilt of violins

mellow moonglow
glimmering over
freshly fallen snow

a bugbit maple leaf
a pale pink columbine

I want to grasp and hold
the glint and shine of
sunlight on the lake

that look I've known
in loving eyes

to never let them go
to own and keep them
evermore enshrined.

Not possible.
Impossible.
It cannot be.

Why even now
I fall in love again

with you

impossibly.

Ruins of Dawn

the morning after
we have had words – the sea is
in a cup of tea

almost the sound of falling
a tear on a piece of toast

Sonetto Primavera

Love, I do not love you more in spring
when every green thing boldly sprouts
new blades and the old dogwood touts
plump promises of pinkwhite blossoming –

my love for you needs no awakening –
it's grown in every season: flood and drought,
the stun of cold, the wilt of heat. Within, without.
I do not love with less than everything.

Still, there is a quickening in spring my heart
can sense, can see – as if a blackwhite photograph
turned gracefully to hues of flame and sun and sky;

it stirs my love for you – my fully seasoned art –
to a fresh colour, a brief dance, a song, a laugh
that fools me once again without my knowing why.

Sonetto Timoroso

Upon a sea of doubt in love I drift
Knowing I do not know the way to go
When torrents take my craft so swift
Toward you – I am a boat I cannot row.

So many moons surround you that my own
Pale beam adds little to your light.
Were I to make my tender feelings known
I fear you would be – oh so graciously – polite.

Stark reality could break my heart
Sooner than love lived only in a dream,
So I will keep my distance, and my life apart
From you, in silent ardor and esteem.

Love knows not how it grows or why,
Nor, in my utter helplessness, do I.

Part Two

As Far as Sicily

Future Perfect

We did not plan
aloud or far ahead
knowing how the envy of the gods
(as that of man) is
easily aroused. We dreaded
ruining our odds.

We did, however, dream
asleep, awake
of moving on to something more –
from milk to cream
dry bread to honey cake
an after better than before.

We meant more life
just down the road.

Until the universe arranged
an otherwise, a knife
to heart, one morning to explode.
You died, and all was changed.

Instead of dreaming now
alone I let life simply be
the in and out of breath.

I greet its beauty, but allow
no wishful thought, no certainty

except, of course, for death.

Patient Belongings

As if you owned nothing
but a pair of earrings,
the two gold hoops that once hung
from the lobes of your living ears

now occupied a little plastic box
marked "patient's belongings"
someone left for me to find
on the still, hard mound of your chest.

No sign of your cobalt blue kimono
or the brand new underwear
you had been saving in a drawer
and asked me to fetch for you –

my hands shaking – once we knew
the ambulance was on its way.
We lost connection after that.
They came, and you were gone.

Your earrings and I,
with only the turned-off machines
pushed back against the walls to overhear

said our appalling last goodbye. Then
stunned to a disbelief way beyond sorrow,
we went home. In time

I gave the earrings to your sister –
as you know she is a fool for jewelry –
who felt they should be hers.

Most of your other things have gone,
piecemeal, over the years,
each time tearing at the heart.

Only your favorite flannel shirt
stays in the closet still,
its empty arms hanging by its sides,

a last most patient belonging,
waiting for its purpose
to be once again fulfilled.

Into Something Rich and Strange

This small sack of fragments now
is all we have of you: dust and bones.
Today we take it to the sea, allow
a freedom greater than you've ever known.

The ship's captain tells us you may go
as far as Sicily, full fathom five,
by Christmas, going with the flow.
You'll love that, as you would have done, alive.

So we release you to the waves. We watch
you splay to water-fireworks. We toss
sunflowers after you, as on that spot
a single gull floats over our loss.

We cling, returning landward, to an afterglow.
Much easier to believe it must be so.

Bereft

Some mornings I awaken with wet eyes;
tears precede my opening to the light.
I'm in a place I do not recognize
at first, my head still cowebbed by the night.

Deep shadows want to pull me back
to mindlessness, deep soft and gray.
I am an overwrought, limp gunnysack
too tired to lug into another day.

To have to reimagine this old haunt
that was our world – to touch, to walk around
our furniture estranged – so desperately to want
yet lack the sense of being homeward bound:

these are the courages I must begin,
to live a story you're no longer in.

Crepuscule

Name this light a kind of tinting
Between dark and day, a mauve
Interwoven with blue heaven
Hovering over the yew grove.

Always did we keep this hour
Special in our home: your chair,
My chair, sherry on the table
By the gabled window there...

We would look out on new tulips
Then the trumpet vine and phlox
Then nasturtiums and then nothing
But white winter as we talked.

Souls we shared and spoken truly,
Trusting we could lay them bare
In the care of cherished friendship
Which was ours rich and rare...

But a sadness lurks in twilight
Seeks a help to see it through
Wants a lullaby for dying
Needs a loving rendezvous.

So I shudder now at gloaming,
Gloom and dusk – one and the same,
Same two chairs, one glass for sherry
And an ache without a name.

Dumbfounded

dumbfounded is a place
cut like a chasm in the gut
a sharp and instant color of
the space between two moments
dark and seeming without cause

one goes there not by choice
but as the pawn of psychopomps
whose garbled voices suddenly
make clear demands from under
customary drapes of gauze

then nothing is the same
not the piano or a slice of bread…
to breathe is stunning…one cannot
remember the cat's name…one moves
slowly like a walking bruise

who said time heals all wounds?
who said time wounds all heels?
it matters not…with time the place
dumbfounded turns to so much sand
easily shaken from the shoes

Unfallen Rain

Dog days, a wearisome unfallen rain
hangs in the air, a glum unfallen rain.

The slow buzz of fat bees is caught
in flower throats, can't thrum unfallen rain.

Clouds hoard spoils they've taken from the seas,
refuse all pleas to overcome unfallen rain.

Oppression snuffs out every breath – no argument
remains against this deaf and dumb unfallen rain.

Don't move, this too shall pass, we say,
for all the fallen have known some unfallen rain.

A heavy, angry god of thunder booms,
collecting in his kettledrum unfallen rain.

And you, Cynthia, would break this hold of grief?
As if mere words could summon falling rain!

Love's Not Time's Fool

The wheel turns once again to this:
the image of your going
that appalling, horrid yesterday.
Old wounds stir beneath their scars
memories of anguish, fear, and disarray –
the sudden darkness
of your life's closing parenthesis.

Yet anniversaries are not required
for our in memoriam –
let those who think so
take their yearly flowers to your grave.
They'll soon forget again. They do not know
the way you visit constantly
as earth, the air, the water, fire …

as reminding, unseen amulet,
as the in-dwelling, the abruptly
disappearing dream at dawn,
the little pause over a cup at noon,
the lengthening shadow on the lawn –
in the gut-pull of gravity,
split-second, as each sinking sun is set.

Sunflowers

Sunflowers crowd the driveway
their big round faces

gawking incredulity
like children grown too tall too fast.

Seeded in March to become in August
the reminders of a memory, top heavy

now they stand for one who loved them
specially, who gave them meanings –

"leave some for the birds," and
"this good oil will heal," and
"Fermat's spiral is a golden ratio," and
"always seek the light" –

who herself became, too far, too fast
a memory. Too soon the after of before.

Sunflowers in the driveway cannot know
they mean all that, and more. Much more.

Real Estate

This was our house.
Now it is mine alone.
It is a good house, warm, with lovely bones
and flowers all around. But
it is oddly empty now, and also full
of too much memory. The past
crowds in like those loud crows I hear
competing for the roadkill down the street.

Archive of disappearing dreams, defeat,
silenced laughter, unsat chairs,
old discs nobody wants to play,
books likely to remain unread and
many, many papers I must shred –
like any good museum it requires
maintenance, archival care. But
time has worked its own perverse repair:

what was once so dear and so familiar
has been slowly turning strange.
A kind of mercy has arranged it so
love is no longer of this house.
Has love grown lesser? No.
It has grown lighter and more
portable. It lives and moves wherever
heart and mind may chance to go.

Sonetto Incredulo

There used to be a wish for your return
here in my heart, a craving for your smile
so I could bask in it again, a little while
and know the worthiness for which I yearn –

the love you brought, that taught me to unlearn
all anger, sadness, sense of alien exile
and know a place where we together could beguile
from seeming ashes, embers, constancy of burn.

But so much grief has been, and change,
a certain strangeness I believed could never be
has crept into my unbelief and now seems true:

you would not want this world, so rearranged
by time, which once so cruelly stole you from me,
and now, incredibly, is stealing me from you.

The Sun Also Sets

Without a bedtime story or a lullaby
the evening's blush sinks to a deeper red
then slips into a slit between the earth and sky
leaving our goodbyes lingering, unsaid.

I do not want to go, or let you go.
I want to dare this ending, call its bluff,
delay our parting with a sudden overflow
of words – too many and yet not enough –

while you, my dearest one, would choose
blunt disappearance, the mute way
to stanch an agony – those deeper blues
along the skyline fire – as if to say

the sun rises, the sun also sets.
So let it set. Let us let it. Let's.

Sung Exhortation to my Heart, in the Shower

'Tis of thee, 'tis of thee, 'tis of thee,
of thee I sing, sweet heart,
my pith, my mind, my core,
my courage and my *coeur de chant*.
We are the whole damn chorus coming down
raining sad songs for all the weary world.
My tympanist, my diastolic, my systolic dance,
my own hell-heaven, coloratura and my profundo.
Let's sing our opera in Italian so
we move ourselves to tears, and join the flow…

che faro senza Euridice?
dov' andro senza il mio ben?

Sweet heart of many gratis blessings,
passion and compassion when they come,
only hum for one more time the aria

piu succorso, piu Speranza
ne d'al mondo, ne d'al ciel….

but please, dear heart, don't go with Orfeo.
Don't break.
Let singing be ablution, water be the gift of tears.
Let memory remain where it belongs–
only a part of the wholehearted song.
And let us rise out of this place –
grab a towel now, begin to climb –
into the wilderness and music of emerging time.

The Palpable Obscure

All souls own this evening, love,
blurring borders between quick and dead.
And even if the fearsome moans of man
did not appoint this time as hallowed,
our backyard trees announce it, as they
lose their glory and become their bones.

The veil is at its thinnest now, that
suddenly obscured you and left me
bereft, dumbfounded in the desolately clear.
Once a day, at least, I stop to wonder
where you are. I do not think of
you as being here. Except, tonight

a heightening of powers in the darkness
wants to break November from October
with a cold slap and a small wail in the wind.
Something more than me, something much
more sure that you abide, this night, brings
you, in ways that I can almost touch.

Part Three

The Job of Watching Snow

Riviera Reverie

A whole wall of windows to the southeast of
the house allows the sun abundant access

to a green-serene, high-ceilinged room
where trapezoids of light fall on the carpet

and invite the family animals to bask.
Here comes the dog, in search of parking space.

Being of great size – no sunny patch
will be quite large enough – she is obliged to spin

until her blind man's buff causes
the twirl itself to choose if head or rump

will lie in shade. Dog decision made,
the girl cat sidles perilously close,

squints left, then right, then nonchalantly
stretches to a lounging mass of legs and fluff.

The boy cat, all noblesse oblige,
takes his reserved, tacitly acknowledged place.

Drawn to their warm, imaginary blankets
spread upon the floor, these beloved creatures

bring to mind the worshipful habitués
of Côte d'Azur, Côte d'Or. As the sun reaches

they respond, grab on, luxuriate
and, for this brief moment, even teach.

Should a phone call come for any one of them
I'll say they are away, gone to the beach.

Lulu, Snow Watcher

she was a dumpster digger
of an undetermined age
a little strumpet left
to cruise the city streets
hurting fighting dirty

when a trumpet-playing hand
in the Salvation Army band
lifted her up from misery
took her to shelterland

"Hallelujah" was the name we
gave her when we took her home
we cleaned her double paws
we fed her fish and love and
just plain "Lulu" she became

not cute not pretty she is
small and oddly beautiful
a true fur person of droll
asymmetrical black markings
on a fluffy coat dull gold
strangely short-legged
with wise yellow eyes
mooting the question whether
felines really do have souls

since winter's come she has
the job of watching snow

leaving her customary station

on the piano by the metronome
she jumps to a wide windowsill
as soon as flakes begin to fall

there she remains a sentinel
until snow stops she simply
stares quite statuesquely still

it's harder now with getting old
yet there's a grit about her
watching there – like a survivor
pondering a once-known time
or place where it was very cold

Cat Watching Snowfall

Such cold and kindly happening
is worthy of full attention.
At least the cat thinks so.
What does she know? She's only
a lump of golden fur on a red rug
sitting immobile, mesmerized
by motion on the other side of glass,
a constancy of flakes falling
soundlessly to the white earth.

What does she know of consequences
difficult for drivers of our trucks and cars,
for keepers of the fire, for bones
whose trembling tells their skin
that they should be in Florida?
Maybe all the cat can know is
absentmindedness about these things.

Maybe she is seeing only visions
of a world of only happening
where sorely needed softness
sometimes falls for hours on end;
where, if you should look
most deeply into weather, you
might sometime see a friend.

Vigilante Farm

The Rumford Falls Times tells
of a man at Vigilante Farm under
a photo of him, carrying feed on his back,
with five piglets following beside, behind.

(They might be thinking, if pigs do think,
adorations of the man. Not for his mind
but what he carries in his sack.)

The Times tells how the man's
made sure he would not love
or grow attached. He named the piggies
Breakfast, Lunch, Dinner, Supper, Snack.

They follow him, headed out of the photo
into the newsprint, unconcerned,
blinded by love. His name is
Sack of Food on Back.

More's the Pity

The sheep have flocked to the water's edge
and now they weep
not knowing how to swim.

Above them in the usual skies, a crow
caws mockingly:
Fools! You were herded here by lies!

But now the sheep have come to love
the melodrama of
their bleating cries. Don't judge, wallow

in the comfort of a group-think nudge.
Sheep will be sheep –
still, it's hard to sympathize.

In the Cards

I'll tell you where the dog died,
said the woman, meaning
nothing could be put over on her.

Here we call it like it is.
No use wasting breath
trying to convince a body otherwise.

A spade is a spade. A heart
cannot be bought with diamonds
or a club. Right here

is where the dog died. We
buried it in the back yard.
Whatever you have to say: shut up.

Equinox

The toad shook off two snowy
eyebrows with a sudden twitch.
Mud shivered in the blowy
balm, rippled the juicy ditch.
Toad popped its eyes awake,
tapped by a warm green witch
and listened for the snake
between the lines, between
the woods and the lip of the lake.

The snake wiped itself clean
against a brand new blade
of grass, and practiced looking mean.
Scales, skin newly-made,
wet with excitement and tight
on the courage of the unafraid,
tongue flapping a small red kite,
snake kept its body low
in wait, and saved its bite.

The toad, heavy and slow
with eggs, had to cross the line
between new waters and old snow.

How could a snake pine
sentimentally for what
its gut demanded by design?

Snake brain cracked like a nut.
Coiled venom, raging spit
leapt from the rut

and took the toad, near all of it
into the mouth. But deep
the toad moan would not fit
nor drift to easy sleep
down in the snake. It caught high
in the maw, swimming to keep

alive. The monster that followed
was dreadful to see, as it tried
to get into, get out of, the hollow –

a birth in reverse, blaming the sky
for being unable to swallow
for being unable to die.

Last Cat's Conundrum

Where did everybody go, do you suppose?
I thought I had them counted, every nose
going about its business everyday –
dog in the grass, cats in their litter tray;
now eat, now sleep – precise punctilios.

It started when one of the ones who wear the clothes
left us, went wherever someone goes
who never comes again. That's when I began to say
where did they go?

Later on, my brother cat lay down and froze
in a forever sleep. There was such weeping; flows
of tears like rivers. Then, oh, no! The dog fell prey
to that inscrutable. I feel as if I'm yesterday,
trying to know, waiting for my eyes to close –
where did everybody go?

Part Four

Poetry These Days

Poetry These Days

If a poem is about a cat
many come to read and love
one of the truest loves they know.

If a poem is about a river
or the ocean or a sunset
interest is sure to grow.

If a poem artfully confesses
a deep yearning or a wound,
many gather to console –

if it surfs toward sex
the text is dropped
for a lace camisole.

But if it's just about a stark
unsentimental basic loneliness
grasping a truth by metaphor

chances are its limits
may be transcendental
but mean nothing at the bar.

A Fib

A Fibonacci sequence

Oh
yeah?
Really?
You think so?
This is a poem?
Then I am Marie Antoinette
driving a purple corvette as I text this vignette!

International Radiotelephony Spelling Alphabet Soup

It seems that ALFA, betting
she would always be the first in line
said BRAVO to herself and

CHARLIE her sweet valentine
took her to the DELTA where
a conchy band called ECHO

played a sexy FOXTROT
and the vino was con secco.

Meanwhile at the GOLF course
near a big luxurious HOTEL
in INDIA, JULIET had found a KILO of

old LIMA beans that had begun to smell
and she asked MIKE for counsel
but he really didn't care

he was too worried that NOVEMBER
was approaching with its frigid air

and what would OSCAR his poor
PAPA do stuck up there in QUEBEC
the poor old ROMEO

without a credit card or cheque
pining for the warm SIERRA
where once he danced the TANGO

with some woman that he met who
 wore a UNIFORM the color of a mango.

So no one was the VICTOR in the end
they all drank too much WHISKEY
and took off for Honolulu…

besides who really needs
an X-RAY just to tell

a YANKEE from a ZULU?

Sapphics

Let eleven syllables dance on feet of
language music, all in a line together
keeping true to life in the heart and bright with
feminine endings.

Prelude to a Necessary Song

Are they trying to be songs,
those small urges nudging the heart
toward the throat, wanting to live on air?

Very like songs they are,
fragments of song, ideas for a song
swimming upstream to a belonging

with mute swans on the clear
mirror of a mountain lake
gliding toward the inevitable.

But what if they're off-key?
Sung wrong? What indeed.
Try to remember what

someone looking for the lost chord
midway up a mountain in Tibet
said, and which I pass along:

a bird does not sing
because it has an answer;
it sings because it has a song.

Part Five

The Child Inside

The Trick of Treats

Beware the trick of treats, my little one,
of sugary ideals, of endless halcyon

as you go forth this hallowed eventide
your begging pleasure bag held open wide

go not oblivious, bewitched into oblivion.

Candy corn spits from a saw-toothed gun
marshmallow ghosts devour a skeleton

behind your mask's deceit remain clear-eyed:
beware the trick of treats.

This world's a mixing bowl of bleak and fun
of up and down, of swapping rain and sun

two one-eyed tadpoles circling inside
give a close chase that's never satisfied

and bitters dwell with sweets, my little one,
beware the trick of treats.

Sticks and Stones

*Sticks and stones may break my bones but words
will never hurt me. ~a maxim for children*

Poor Charlie felt he had the right
to be as hateful as he might;
that's freedom of expression.
He travelled with the savvy smart,
was good with words and graphic art;
they polished his aggression.

It's not as if he didn't know
his wit dished out a hurtful blow;
such was his intention.
He called it satire, an old trick
of literary rhetoric
to mask his condescension.

"Watch your mouth," his father said,
but Charlie self-expressed instead;
wise warnings were ignored.
His righteousness, he came to think,
with drafting pen and colored ink
more potent than a sword.

Those on the receiving end
of Charlie's penchant to offend
stewed in this juice.
A self-expression more inclined
toward the body than the mind
let loose.

The awful consequences came
in retribution with a claim
on Charlie's head.
Aggression had begotten more
aggression, evening the score.
Now Charlie's dead.

"Sticks and stones
may break my bones,"
still rings the schoolyard cry,
"but words will never hurt…"
we also still assert,
and that…is just a lie.

The Child Inside

In the belly of all beginning, big as a pea, is the child inside;
rolling salt of the spume, of tears, of the sea, is the child inside.

The trouble with floating? Habits accrue against floating, they
grow like barnacles, heavy, sinking the glee of the child inside.

The dark in a stranger much older, much larger, manipulates,
teaches a sorrow, impresses a dark tyranny on the child inside.

Replace the true face, deface with tattoo, learn what to do, and
for others change or cover the caged agony of the child inside.

Even the seemingly suave may be suddenly taken with urges
unkempt to disrupt Miss Manners At Tea, by the child inside.

A tiny detector of bogus, though paused or muted at times,
still writhes against snake oil and hyperbole in the child inside.

Call me by name, please notice I came, I was here
I am me!...persists the perennial plea of the child inside.

Toddle first, toddle last, time siphons the juice from the bloom;
still there, still at work, is the sweet bumble-be of the child inside.

Are We There Yet?

Are we there yet? – comes the restless cry
of bouncing children in the car's back seat.
No, darlings, we will get there by and by

comes from a front-seat grownup in reply.
Before too long, the rigmarole repeats:
are we there yet? – now a plaintive cry

much louder and annoyingly pitched high.
Again the answer, in a tone now not so sweet:
sit down, be quiet; we will get there by and by.

There is nothing for it but to lie back, sigh
and take a nap or find some munchables to eat.
Are we there yet? – a forbidden, useless cry.

Staring out the window, a daydreaming little eye
watches the road, the trees, advance, retreat
in endless tickings toward the by and by –

it would inquire of a power in the passing sky
with no one else to hear, unvoiced, discreet –
are we there yet? Then in a whimper, not a cry,
say to itself: just wait until I get there, by and by.

Is It Christmas Yet?

The pine tree, wounded
bright, has come into the house
to die, standing up.

Sleep My Little Cabbage

Now the making will unmake
And the sewing will unsew;
How long will the longing take
'Til the letting will let go?

Fais do-do, fais do-do
Mon p'tit chou si doux, si beau.

Falling dark must surely fall,
The slow blowing will unblow;
Walls of safety will unwall,
Cradle rock unto, unfro.

Fais do-do, fais do-do
Mon p'tit chou si doux, si beau.

Good-bye comes to be ungood
As the hello's unhello;
Missing is misunderstood,
Knowing's clouded to unknow.

Fais do-do, fais do-do
Mon p'tit chou si doux, si beau.

Broken heart will not unbreak,
Wish will not make go ungo,
So, my little cabbage cake
Take my love, now, fais do-do…

Fais do-do, fais do-do
Mon p'tit chou si doux, si beau.

Part Six

There Were No Stars

That Memory

I do not need to summon that one –
it returns to me as regularly as the valleys
in between the hills. There's Mum again
sorting laundry, one eye to whatever's
boiling over on the stove. The latest baby
has awakened, cries like toothache. Probably
needs changing. Is that someone at the door?

And where am I? Slouched on the couch
reading yet another story of some other life.
Suddenly she's there, Mum looming over me
and a hard whack smacks across my face:
"Who do you think you are? Get your nose
out of that book! Make yourself useful!" Why,
I wonder, is her voice so crazy, full of hate?

As suddenly, she's gone. I am ten years old.
Big red drops fall to the open page upon my lap.
Swallowing blood, I raise my arm and dab my
nose upon my sleeve, lean my head back to
stop the flow. What will I tell the old librarian
about these stains that happened to her book?
I stand, a little wobbly. Go and help. Only later

do I see how certain words like Love and True
began to grow unmeaningful that day. Poetry
slipped quietly away. Usefulness ate the better
part of time until, after half a dozen decades of
the kind of sweet obedience that kills, in age I find
poetry again, sufferance, compassion to forgive –
though Mum is dead, and that old memory still lives.

Epistemology

They never should have shown me
those pictures: the man who
wore a long white robe, sandals,
his moist brown eyes always looking up,
his long silk hair surrounded by a mist of gold.

They told me it was he who changed the world.
He spoke wise words but never wrote them down.
With time I learned he was the one
who saved me. From what, I did not know.
He had to be killed in order to do it.

After that, no robe, no sandals.
Nearly naked, limp hair matted,
head hung low, he was nailed
to a hideous wooden cross. I was
too young to not look, to not listen.

I put the pictures, the story, the cross
away in a deep place where
things never let go. Even though
all of it happened when I wasn't there.
Nor was anyone who told me so.

Ravelry

it reminds me of Imelda
the beloved elder who
held my pudgy mitts
to needles and to yarn
to show me how
before I knew what for

it moves in steady rhythm
creates loops and knots
that hold together
do not brag but build
a keepsake and by touch
may tell sometimes of love

it is a zen
for western minds
old fuddy fashioned
an annoyance and
anachronism
to a world all thumbs

its text
the texture of a fabric
danced not twiddled
coaxed into patterns
of a mathematics
music understands

it is an ethic and
a discipline made

from the sun
the clouds
the grazing sheep
in fields below

gathered and woven
strand to strand
as they become
a cap or muffler
mittens made to warm
a pair of human hands

To Bear the Beams of Love

And we are put on earth a little space,
that we may learn to bear the beams of love…
~Songs of Innocence and Experience, William Blake

After all, wasn't it the wanted thing,
this sudden basking in a golden beam,
being one on whom the sun would seem
to rise and set? For whom whole choirs sing?

In those long hours of heaven's opening
only to pour upon each cherished dream
bleak rain, or that grey dampening stream
of dullness, dim and witless threatenings –

what was the hope, the hap, so striven for?
Simply to see the end of suffering? Or was it
something more? These beams of love burn,

smooth as lasers, loosen the stuck door;
delicate, precarious gold haze fuzzes
the soul – reveals a whole world to unlearn.

There Were No Stars

There were no stars, or I remember none;
no evidence or inkling night or day.
Unless I'm forced to count the sun,
which never lit anyone's way

but indiscriminately spilled upon the fuss
of things, goading as equals, good and not,
to race, to chase after the same bus
which never ever could be caught.

I was immersed in city time, heaven obscured
by lowering, by thickening of air.
Was it Elizabeth the poet who assured
about the stars "they're there, they're there…"?

I did not even think to look.
And what good would another's knowing
do for me? My nose was always in a book
so I could hardly see where I was going.

The Food That Feeds but Does not Satisfy

The food that feeds but does not satisfy
emerges as from seeds I did not sow
and like a rampant weed it starts to grow
until there's not a plot it does not occupy.

It is a carnival aroma, cotton candy, fries,
a siren song, a laughing braggadocio
a knowingness that doesn't really know –
the more I eat, the more it multiplies.

Hour by hour I fear how it devours my day
in ways that warrant constant connectivity
first thing in the morning and the last at night.

Otherwise it is invisible, a marvel of hearsay
that shows me pictures I can't help but see
and sends me sounds by radio and light.

In truth the urge to fight
an appetite for eating that which eats me is absurd
as is the name Wi-Fi, which is a nonsense word.

It rides not on the wings of birds
but baffling things that fly and perch at will.
Whose will? A question to be answered still.

Things They Are Throwing Out That I Would Rather Keep

The little women's college
where we little women went.

A nephew's obligation to
say thank you for the gift I sent.

The courtesy of titles, surnames,
when addressing people you don't know.

Predominance of substance
over show.

That public is what everyone
and private is what no one sees.

Books made from trees.

Bing Crosby

Choosing among apples at the supermarket
just the other day I heard
Bing Crosby singing "Jingle Bells".
Background music so I'm told
can motivate a buyer in a store.
But Bing? Bing Crosby? This must be

the day marked shopping day for us
I say to a green pyramid of Granny Smiths.
And sure enough here comes a busload
slowly from the home for seasoned citizens.
I doubt the muzak moves them any faster
though most likely they'll remember Bing.

Bing Crosby, ah, Bing Crosby,
how you crooned and nanna swooned
in nineteen-fifty-something –
how you spun inside the gramophone
seventy-eight revolutions per minute
dreaming of a White Christmas just like

the ones you used to know. Was that how
I came to think of Christmas mostly as a longing?
Strange and difficult to satisfy. I try
to re-create the pleasures of the past
(and leave the woundings out), but it's a task
unfestive, one I'm loath to be about.

All I hear are someone's memories.
All I see grows gaudier, each year
more desperate to enforce the thing.

All I want is willingness to let the night be dark
(except for stars), dear friends, these apples
red and green, and (maybe) just a bit of Bing.

Last Evening, At Supper

who wondered who
sat in my place that moment
there among the passing
soup bowls
plates of prawns –

whose head was bowed for grace?

above the oaken board
the wine, the bread,
a waft of tarragon
married the onion's pungency
in a half-lit phenomenon of
dread that I could not retrace

the hand lifting my spoon
looked like my grandma's hand –
how did that happen?
when?
she is long gone

am I living her again?

companions became colored fog
and I heard nothing that was said
around the room
until –
napkins wiping mouths –

the noisy
pushing back of chairs

the rattling plates on plates
the crumbs
the broom

Fourth of July

The night sky is bright
bursting with chrysanthemums
of fire, crackling light –

I watch them fall to darkness
not feeling independent.

Return to a Landscape

This morning north
and east of what
was once my home,
the dusky mountains
trace their frozen
undulations mystified
against a salmon sky.
In the middle distance
cozy little houses
tuck themselves among
deep mounds of snow,
exhaling from their
brick red chimneys
all I know
of them or theirs.
Nearby the pointed firs
point up, to pointlessness
through January air.

Nowhere is home.
So home is everywhere.

Part Seven

Palimpsest

By the Time You Wake up,
Your Hair Will be White

…you will own the biblical hoary head. Your
tree will know how oddly a branch may grow to
sapless, brittle treachery. Fear alone will
threaten to break it.

Most of those who loved you are dead. Their absence
shadows, haunts remembering. No one living
slows to listen really or hear your story.
If you should tell it.

Breath of the morning, beautiful new forgiveness,
not a thought to limit or change or end it –
noon afire with promises, now a rush to
flushingly spend it –

all will come to evening. You are not of
your time; you *are* your time. A shutter
opens, closes, light on a nervous moth-wing
fluttering briefly.

All Over Again

Seems like Beelzebub's winning all over again,
smugly cavorting and grinning all over again.

God and the weather are angry and threaten us now.
Adam and Eve must be sinning all over again.

Who will be Noah and notice a need for an Ark?
The number of righteous is thinning all over again.

Flames lick the eaves, acrid smoke rips the nose,
and Nero has come violining all over again.

Now to earth's wanderers who will give refuge and
make them at home with her spinning all over again?

We say that we love, we want to believe it, but
why does it feel like tailspinning all over again?

The proverbs of ancients hammer our latter-day
numbskulls with dire disciplining all over again.

It was all said before but since nobody listens –
must we go back to beginning all over again?

Palimpsest

The earnest monastery scribe begins
to scrape: he must expunge, obliterate
a text of Archimedes. Tonsured pate
bowed over parched and pumiced skins,
stone bench stone-cold, to his chagrin
hemorrhoids, indigestion complicate
his task. But laborare et orare, so he meditates;
offers up his troubles in atonement for his sins.

Beyond clerestory walls descendent sheep
are growing new skins in a lilac breeze.
Fra Pennafolio envies how they graze
oblivious, while lately he's been losing sleep
fighting dark avengers of Hippocrates.
For help, he rubs his cabochon of chrysoprase.

He must not let it faze him.
After all, in frugal fact, parchment is dear
and perfect skins are rare. He must persevere,
erase and rewrite without fear.
It is a holy labor, surely in the angels' care,
to cleanse away the pagans for a book of prayer.

A Great Reckoning in a Little Room

Of Christopher Marlowe

It could have been a little room like this –
four walls, a window, table, chair – tales
tell us he was stabbed and cursing when he died
a much regretted master of blank verse...

but that was long ago and this is now
in this little room, at this window
looking out upon the ruddy repetitions
of a blank brick wall across the way...

I count poetic feet by heart, bemoan
the calling of them, just as that Touchstone
who held a plumb line for The Bard:
"When a man's verses cannot be read
nor a man's good wit seconded...
it strikes a man more dead than
a great reckoning in a little room," he said.

Even the graffitist, wily, undercover,
come by night to paint his colors on the wall
might lurk in shadowy corners come the dawn
to overhear effects of his calligraphies

or the forest with the falling tree and no one
there to hear – does it find the earthy thump
insisted by an inner ear dwelling in thought?

It all comes down to one small room
and looking out the window wondering why
why embark upon an expedition or ambition
surely doomed to disappointment or despair?

Wisdom has said: because it's there.
Then, too, there is that falling tree…anything
to get out from under it, sound or no sound,
purely by dead reckoning, no guarantee.

The Old Guitarist

A painting by Pablo Picasso (1903/04)

His pale blue bones bend
graciously, fragile as fossils
round the place of song

blue is the very world
that grounds him, clothes him
in arrest against blue stone;

blinded eyes shut out
all but his vision of
impending things; they fall

into the hole of the guitar
where his limp thumb plucks
beauty out of tightened strings.

Pablo gave us this old man
when pitiful and melancholy
were the palette's only colors

and a gessoed tabletop
the only panel ready to receive
the pentimento of his pain.

This is what it comes to,
the blue painting seems to say,
a blindness, poor and old and

left to suffer homeless
in a world of monochrome
under a dome bereft of stars.

Cold, cold, except for one
dear possibility, colored warm –
the promise of a butternut guitar.

The Tribes Are Wondering

Maybe in their bones or late-night thoughts
the leaders wonder how it ends,
how it began, how one can answer
to and fro the dark. Maybe

the wondering is very small,
a moment between this and that,
stopped in a window just above the sink.
Summer shivers. Snowball disappears in snow.

Who is leader, really, who is led?
A wonderment, though no one lets another
know he doesn't know.
Puffed chests and roasted turkeys

to grandmother's house we go.
The motions are protected by a blanket
covering a blank. The young are puzzled
as to why, or who to thank.

In a Garden of Givens

They are not mean, but meaning to be kind,
the ones whose work it is to bring him here –
merely a job to do, to hold and steer
an old man who is frail, half-blind,
toward a sunny bench where he may find
companionship in leafy atmosphere –
perhaps a little bird to tweet some cheer
and take him out of his own mind.

Here, everything is new under the sun:
the spill of light climbs up a tree
a little breast of sand temples the ants
a chickadee bows like a tiny nun
upon a branch, to hear the pink soliloquy
of a wild rose, dressed for the dance.

All is circumstance.
Seated between mirth and agony
no longer wishing to foresee
no longer slave to memory
his ancientness, still as a garden gnome,
waits for whoever comes to fetch him home.

Obligatory Wake

One after another, those of the condolence queue,
wearing whatever passes now for Sunday clothes,
snake across the chapel carpet to review
the body. Say how sorry. Look morose.
Those of the right religion stop and kneel.
Some even reach to touch the corpse, who dare
to know how a dead hand might feel,
then cross themselves and murmur a small prayer.
A parish priest arrives to lead the rosary;
the lapsed, the unbelievers, sneak out for a smoke.
Who sent which flowers? We must nose and see.
A distant relative retells his funeral joke.
At ten the undertaker flashes lights.
Everyone leaves. Nobody says goodnight.

A Crow Upon a Dead Tree Branch

Where does a thought go when it is forgotten? ~ Sigmund Freud

when a thought is forgotten
where does it go?
take for example the thought of
a crow upon a dead tree branch –

on the way to forgotten
suppose it turns to vulcanite
then Vulcan's godly fire
then to a lover's face in candle light
before it sputters to blank indigo –

does it then drown as if
swept by a riptide or an undertow
to distances or deep below the rushed
oncoming waves of other thoughts?

drowned and yet not dead
as zero is not nothing
a place-holder in a place
so low as to seem bottomless –
the past as embryo?

this much we know:
though it may sleep for eons
it awaits a resurrection –
there is every chance it will
return unbidden unexpectedly

upon a dead tree branch – a crow

Part Eight

Keeping Keeping On

The Air

steady, steady
the air
is rich
and stout –
and if we laugh
the air
goes rushing
out

steady, steady
the air
is hungry
thin –
and if we weep
the air
comes rushing
in

Griselda

She of the dark battle
enters this downtrodden day

unbidden she steals in
upon the windblown cold,
rides on a window's rattle
creeps along the weather of dismay.

She wants to grasp, get hold
and sink her talons deep

into the tender places
stir and rouse the vicious
powers of the soul
much better left asleep.

Who can answer why
she comes and sometimes stays

or how to steer a fragile craft
adrift and trembling toward
her perfect reasons
and her empathetic sighs

around the urge to simply and
forever slip away.

Cold Comfort

Worst days tilt underfoot.
Ground and moorings sway. Tentatively
now we grasp into the fog
to ever deeper gray.

Smudged edges lose the old horizon
that so helped our keeping keeping on.
We are so rained upon.
What could the gods be thinking?

Times like this I conjure sight and sound
from wisdom old and vulgar new:
the rats are still around
which means the ship's not sinking.

Let Nothing You Dismay

God rest ye merry, gentlemen,
let nothing you dismay. ~ *18th century carol*

Though morning comes again
as grim as gray as dim as
a blank wish to crawl back into bed
and start again some other day,
let nothing you dismay.

The giant plastic manger scene
and holiday inflatables now lie
collapsed all limp upon their lawns
as if a scroogey grinchy neighbor
shot them dead as he drove by

but it was likely just the wind,
so adversarial this time of year,
as weather obeys nothing but itself
regardless of a Santa Claus balloon
or Rudolph the red-nosed reindeer.

Just beyond the window
frost has dangled silver
bangles on a piney tree
and just beyond that…fog
so thick there's little else to see.

There's no one here but me
the fog god seems to say…
so rest you gently if not merry;
take a bit of comfort in oblivion,
let nothing you dismay.

February Fill-Dyke

Now is a perplexing
season in-between
the custom quartering of the year –
no bloom, no grow,
no reap, no sow –
the water of the world
collects itself to overflowing
and becomes the atmosphere.

Another drippy morning dawns,
we mutter "not again…"
the paperboy who thumps
his sodden news against the door
looks mad as a wet hen.

The gift of tears has come
to Tefnut, weeping, on her knees.
Damp wads of facial tissue fall
before sad movie after sad
played on our DVDs.

It's February fill-dyke, be it
black or white, the farmers say.

Time for the heavens to let loose
the sins they've taken in. Time
to cry for nothing, night or day.

The Story of the Glory Of

And then the stars
the holy wafer moon
shone glittery, shone full
(was it for just a blink?)

turned midnight to high noon
a nearly swooning madness of
sweet flight before falling
back to black as ink.

And then began the temporal
succession of plain days
soft-slippered slow processions
into comfort and familiar ways

a preference for what
cuts clean the edges of
unruly fringe, a deference
to the well-oiled, silent hinge.

And then the stars
the holy wafer moon
shone quieter, more faraway,
glittering re-tellers of

the story of the glory of
the thing to which we cling
as we get used to almost
(almost) anything.

Between Commercials

A winter draught
plays on the spine,
shiver music
finely cuts
a path into the hair,
the air becomes
an old disease of mind.
Time for
a long walk, large
confessions to the trees,
advice from the trapped
echoes in abandoned shells.
Time for
something pure…
that will not sell,
for emptiness to call upon
a greater emptiness
for cure.

Part Nine

Distracted into Now

It's Madness

…it's madness to live without joy. ~ Czeslaw Milosz

It's madness to live without joy, to will
to wake and look forward to nil,
to drag a dull clod through the day
with little to give or to say,
to keep going nowhere, uphill –

to look out and dream by the sill
of elsewhere and elsewise until
the traveling river has trickled away –
it's madness to live without joy.

Beyond the forest of chill
is a clearing – quiet, sun-filled.
It awaits. Go. Not to pray
but to listen for what to obey.
There'll be things to destroy. Still,
it's madness to live without joy.

A Dog in the Grass

Serene she poses
still as the stone lions
flanking the stone steps
of the public library

just an old black dog
couchant among dandy yellow weeds
and volunteer forget-me-nots
of blessed-virgin blue

who seems to take for granted
all the grassy sweetness
that is possible in spring.

There ought to be a picture of
this moment warmed by sun
faintly redolent of lilac,
gurgling with matins of
a hidden mourning dove –

it should be digitally stunned
for keeps, held like a pungent
stem of timothy between the teeth –

with a camera one could save it
in that little one-eyed crypt
that neither hears nor sees but
registers and stores as holy
relics to recall what's dead.

That being said, the trick is
to stand camera-less
within a spot of sun
just looking, listening, and
smell the lilac, taste the timothy

as moment fades
into another moment – stay
and watch the dog get up,
shake her whole skin, raise
snout to sniff, then trot away.

MaryMartha

She rises from her soft
seat of enjoyment

puts aside her book and shakes
the glimmer from her gaze:

some falls into the rug, some
slips into the corners of her eyes.

This last amount goes into the kitchen
with her so that even after she

arrives,
bends over a cucumber and

begins to slice, she's not entirely
about the business of slicing. Or

if she is about
the business of slicing

it is not a cucumber.

Valediction Spoken in a Melancholy Tone while all Alone at Sunset on a Grassy Knoll in the Presence of Several Quaking Aspen Trees Forbidding Mourning

With apologies to John Donne

O much I liked
what you appeared to be.

So much I came to love
the you I seemed to see.

So much for wishing, wanting
what I fancied to be true.

So much for you.

Should the Ability Appear

Should the ability appear, to read outdoors,
A book rests open on my lap awaiting here
To take me far from fragrant pine and sycamore
Should the ability appear.

But I am hooked, distracted into now, I fear,
Under the influence of lilac, dreaming on a hellebore,
Holding my breath to hear a bobolink draw near.

I've brought a book out in the sun only to ignore
Its poor inked pages while I drink the atmosphere.
I'll still read other worlds – it's what the book is for.
Should the ability appear.

Ode to a Condiment

From the trusty crock you teach
how cold a winter's morning
or how warm a summer's day might be.
Oh not in thermometric numbers by degree
but by your suave substantial answer
to the knife tip's touch,
by your complexion and your spreadability.

At your most noble, taken new
from finest milk and churned
to a consistency all of your own,
epitome of softness and a cache
of flavor – you're unsalted, sweet,
delicately of the pasture: dandelion,
clover or alfalfa, onion grass...

I love yourself
by any means conveyed –
a raft of toast, a lobster tail,
an artichoke sautéed – even my cat
demands a tiny pat of you each day.
But best of all, pièce de resistance,
those days when I bake bread

I break a hunk
warm, before the loaf is sliced,
and slather you all over it.
Then you are paradise.

Six Yellow Tulips

Six yellow tulips stand obliquely
angled on cut stems, sucking up
clean water in a clear glass vase.

They seem to take for granted everything
their tulip ancestors once came to mean –
tulipomania, flower of great price –

seem simply to enjoy their being here today,
chalices raised sacramental to the sun,
opening this morning what they closed last night.

How would a tulip know it took ten years
to make its bulb from seed, or that it still
grows after it is cut and brought inside?

Being eyeless, earless, voiceless, without hands
to do the research, would a tulip ever learn
its name comes from the turban of a Turk?

Only being is a tulip's work. Being
beauty against gloom. After a long winter
being the yellowest, gladdest thing in the room.

An Occasional Poem

For a friend on the occasion of his seventy-something birthday

Now as you approach that swinging door
And think this day you've just arrived, before
You realize you're also leaving seventy and more,
Do not be sad, and do not fear;
You get to keep this number for another year.

What's in a number anyway? No more
Than abstract stuff enough to bore
To songlessness a moody troubadour
Or make a turnip shed a tear
Or take the rooster out of Chanticleer.

No, it's not the numeral that we deplore
But tendencies of an outworn folklore
To make one seem a dinosaur
When it is perfectly, quite clear
To one's own mind: "I'm not as I appear."

In one's own mind, one is eleven evermore:
One day a cowboy, next a sagamore,
Then a young blade barefoot on the shore
Lit up by love, crushed by a cruel sneer.
The feelings do not age, they persevere.

So let us spit the bitter in the cuspidor,
Immortalize the sweetness in a metaphor
And raise our voices in a great "Encore!"
This birthday thing's a time for cheer,
A time for more than one more beer.

And if you come a little bit footsore,
Wearing a birthday suit unlike the one you wore
Into this life – this life that you adore –
So what? You are still you, still dear,
But best of all, you are still here.

Pamplemousse

In darkness I drift
drunk on grapefruit flower air
and give a small hoot
for the lone hooting owl.
The bees all know me by now.

Part Ten

The Way the Sun

By the Androscoggin

The Androscoggin flows, cliff-sheltered,
hidden by a thickness of great pointed firs,
so we cannot see it from our windows
though we know it's there. Sometimes we hear

after a freakish torrent of hard rain
its rushing over rocks – the ones we hop
when crossing – and we're sidelined for awhile.

The local ducks, deer, foxes, skunks
don't seem to mind; they let the river
have its way – grow wider, deeper,

curving slippery as silk over the falls,
roaring down to swirls of sudsy turbulence
then calming to black pools of mystery.

Only the hand that winds the clock of thought,
the sleepless eyes that worry out the window,
know an urge to push the river toward the sea,

while among the firs, small bright eyes
caught on the dark like stars fallen to earth,
watch, and don't agree or disagree.

Conversation with a Creek

I will slap your face
I said
and the water said
go right ahead.

I'll beat you with a stick
I said
and the water said
go right ahead.

I will stomp on you
I said
and the water said
go right ahead.

I'll cut you with my knife
I said
and the water said
go right ahead.

I will nail you in a box
I said
and the water said
go right ahead

as it glittered
in a zillion squints
of dancing glints
along its pebbly bed.

I may be daft
but that was when
I think I heard
the water laugh.

Walking on Water

the cold comes downward
clutching at zero and below
hardening the river's edge
to shims and milky floe

carrying the omen of
the last loon's tremolo

now the rapid river run
must deepen with the chill
grow slower downward
as the alewife also will

under her darkened ceiling
keeping vigilantly still

her ceiling has become
this shining gelid floor
where legged creatures may
step out to gingerly explore

shuffle over it foot by foot
toward the opposite shore

take my hand I hear
on a down-floating feather
and cross now safely
on my ethereal tether

should we slip-fall-drown
we will go down together

January

It is a two-faced god
who keeps this gate,
eyes to see what's gone, what comes

what works through northern nights
as snoring plows clear drifted
passages from there to here

or exhales into humid southern days
the cranky thunderstorms declaring
it is early, it is late.

Beginning is beginning once again –
the gate swings open, Janus grants
another chance, a cleaner slate.

The little wink of possibility
presents itself: all could be more.
The little hiss turns velvety,
whispers: amen, encore…

Downtown, the promise of
perfection has turned heads;
there is a running towards it

on the woodsy paths at dawn
and all along the streets; some
even now, in sweaty rooms, tread

somewhere, doggedly, ahead
ahead, as ground slips
backward underneath their feet.

The Eyes of March

don't dare open the windows yet
though sun pours into the kitchen sink
and warms the cheek like a lover's touch

fill the kettle and do not think
this morning's glimmer is truly gold
for Lenten tendencies tend to break

too suddenly from their prison hold
into a flirty madness that teases
toward a belief that spring has come

a phony fling of warmth that freezes
back into old disappointments of ice
toast the toast for it's only March

posing as April oh so nice
but not yet real so continue to muddle
and wait for the full pink moon to rise

the last potatoes of winter huddle
still deep in the cupboard's dark
making eyes

Fiddleheads

Now that all the windows are open, letting
kindly breezes into the house instead of
shutting out the merciless winds of winter

fiddles are playing.

Under ground they're sounding their strings on fingers;
bows with horsehair stretched to the frog are twinging
whining, sighing strains to a demi-semi –

quavering rhythm.

There, by pebbly pool is a patch of shaded
sod where tiny scrolls have begun to pop up
green and coiled as fine as a bishop's crozier –

fiddleheads! Listen…

chthonic music deep in the earth is playing
waltzes, grand cadenzas, spiccato, thrusting
spirals, pushing songs to the sun, see? Hear them?

Maybe it's me.

New Moon

In paper packets
hundreds of tiny promises lie,
maybe morning glories, maybe cosmos,
awaiting a human act.

Someone has put off
the task of sowing them.
They don't complain.
They dream a shallow trough,

a covering of earth,
some wet, some warmth,
and to express themselves
in a green birth.

Especially today,
the time of the new moon,
(best time to plant
the ancients say)

someone should touch the need
that drives us all,
toward life, the life
in every little seed.

The Way the Sun

The way the sun
creeps over a shoulder
enters, moves about the room

appreciative, accommodating
as a pleasant guest
admiring now this, now that –
the way it warms,

brightens when recognized
the way a cherished friend
after long absence
tenderly is met
with smiling eyes –

the way it's faraway
yet here in hand
today, ethereal gold –

the way this oldest thing
never gets old.

Earth Laughs in Flowers

...Earth laughs in flowers to see her boastful boys
Who steer the plough but cannot steer their feet clear of the
grave...~ Ralph Waldo Emerson, Hamatreya

Just outside my door, a little to the left,
beside the bottom step, I thought I heard
a crocus chuckle from a frost-heaved cleft.

A week or somewhat after that occurred
there was a laugh of daffodils along the pebbly walk.
Later, toting garden tools in my red wagon

how could I ignore those titterings of tulips,
giggling gladioli, snickering snapdragons and
a high-toned tee-hee from a blooming hollyhock?

Was this the earth laughing in flowers to remind
the maker of a private plotting once again
what ultimately is in charge, and what is not?

I shrugged and went indoors, only to find
not peace, not silence, but
the kalanchoe cachinnating in its pot.

Cognac and Emerson, before I went to bed,
made me this dream, from what Ralph Waldo said.

Part Eleven

Let Me Down Easy

To a Tulip

You,
yellow flower
standing in a cobalt vase,
unfurling blades,
stemmed sacramental cup –
winter was hard
but now your simple grace
is green announcement:
things are looking up.
There by the window you
to sunlight are the antiphon,
beauty new as beauties past,
spring's insistence
life should carry on.
Yet you become
most beautiful at last,
when age and death are
what you must fulfill:
come that night
you can no longer
close against the dark,
you open wide until
you are all heart,
and every petal knows
translucence as it falls.
You could be hinting
how to do it, for us all.

What in the World

Dawn, that old hooker light of the world
returns from wherever she spent the night in the world.

Dust motes randomly dance on a yellowish beam,
soft-nudging my dream to a flight from the world.

So much to do…sweep and dust, dust, and it's
dusty again! It feels like a fight with the world.

It's important not to be eaten, at least for today,
or be carried away by the huge appetite of the world.

In their globular bowl, small fry hang among floating
green fronds, hide in the water sprite from the world.

You chocolate mustachioed child, how I love
how your day is another big bite of the world.

Such lucky animals, those who have learned
when to be – and not be – polite in the world.

All of a sudden the day is riddled with hiccups
here as I say once again gesundheit to the world.

One eventually comes to notice the colors of dust –
So many shades between black and white in the world.

I know by a certain color of blue – and also
because we have music, something is right in the world.

Still Life: Maine Oranges

Some places are not
sun-kissed,
that is their very
talent:
to savor the brief
kindness
then gather the slap
inside
and slowly turn it
orange.

Here, where pumpkins
huddle,
bellies touching so
slightly
on the step that needs
a nail,
we watch
the death of summer
ripen,
try to memorize
windfalls
or an amber rain.

It will not be too
long now…
strange isn't it how
orange
the funeral is,
how cold windows
ache with sun.

Hey Nonny

I forget the song, the one for the rain,
and now is a week of wet space.
Hey nonny tell me how it goes again:

the lift in the wing, the spring-tickled brain,
the chuckle through holes in the lace –
I forget those songs, and the one for the rain.

Nose pressed against the cold glass pane,
I have lost Christmas, the child's window face.
Hey nonny tell me how it goes again:

what wind will spin the leaden weather vane,
how can a nothing be erased –
I forget the song, the one for the rain,

the word of magic that will name,
will put a blankness in its place.
Hey nonny tell me how it goes again:

to softly sit and wait for grace.
This I wish, the gift not to complain. But
I forget the song, the one for the rain.
Hey nonny tell me how it goes, again.

In the Shallows

Long thoughts linger in the shallows,
lollygag along the beach
where the tidal waters whisper
lisp and slur their primal speech

where the ebbing wavelets licking
cling a moment to the land
spit their spume, leave little riddles
and blanched shells that suck the sand

edges shift in fickle fractals,
zig damp earth with zags of brine…
though on strolls here in the shallows
bare feet seem to toe a line

as if taunting trekker troopers
swooping seagulls squawk and yell
why is every footstep schlepping
its old burden…parallel?

One quick glance over a shoulder,
the horizon's still out there…
oh, to lightly walk on water
or to gull-glide through the air

perpendicular to margins
on imaginary paths
of green beckoning blue sparkles
above dreadful depths of wrath…

still I turn now, stop in stillness
water clear, ground safe below,
standing easy in the shallows
staring where I dare not go...

there's a staying thing that anchors
to the habits, terror strong,
stronger than the heart's desiring
though desire lives deep and long.

Come September Naturally

Come September
naturally we dry hydrangeas

all those mop-head pompoms
on the ancient hedge that keeps out
strangers like an overbearing mother
to the native sedge along the drive.

Naturally, the timing must be right:
late morning when the dew has dried

on a cool sunny day when blooms
no longer in their prime (not quite passé)
hint at new colors and a bit of stiffening like
paper in the petals gives a mild forewarning.

Catch it now
the ghost still breathing in the flower

whispers to a knowing hand –
strip off my superfluity of leaves then
stand me to repent in crystal water
so my cut stem grieves a bit

until all tears are spent
and I am all evaporated power.

Among Other Things

Among other things
the forsythia blooms
indoors, in water,
just as one presumes –
its tiny yellow openings
burst into day stars
forcing spring
into the winter gloom.

But now the branches
lately cut, are doomed
never to know again
how golden plumes might
ride together on a wind
might bow and swing
among other things.

Separation marks them
for a loamy tomb where
dry sticks end,
sink, are consumed.
Or so it seems, except
for a remembering

a homesickness for sun
an urge toward wings
and what it means to be
a glow in the brume
among other things.

Maple Yellow, Maple Red

Maple yellow, maple red, I see
the killing splendor of your canopy
outside my window as I lie abed
gathering this morning's go-ahead,
whispering this small apostrophe –

how gracefully you ride time's tyranny
and know exactly how to be a tree,
rubrics never read, sermons unsaid,
maple yellow, maple red.

Soon you will die, to some degree,
turn prickly gray as colors flee;
but you'll grow back the brights you shed.
This time next year, I may be dead
while you, most likely once again, may be
maple yellow, maple red.

Another Milestone

For celebration I would go
to a place where I was happy once
where it is possible to dance
three-legged, nice and slow –

or out into deep winter's honest air
where love once walked
and with my stick crack open
every ice-clenched puddle there –

maybe I would haunt the bakery aisle
at Stop & Shop, ogle the cakes,
and scare some people I don't know
with my all-knowing smile.

Forget the presents – my desire
to divest, to simplify, to give away,
and live more quietly a monk-life now
outstrips that old urge to acquire.

So at close of day, a vagrant star
might seem to twinkle loud enough
to seem to ask me how it was
to be here, to have come so far –

I would not know how to reply.
At dusk I would walk home, not
looking back as ice grew once again
on puddles, mirrors to a gridelin sky.

Getting It

For many years you don't get it.
You know you haven't gotten it.
But there's still time and
maybe you'll get it.

You cultivate the persons, places,
things that appear to have it.
What you get there is proof
that you still don't get it.

It's above you, beyond you.
It's all Greek, which you don't speak.
You need more experience,
you need more education.

You need the magic formula,
the password, the key.
You need a teacher, a mentor,
a confidante, confessor, referee.

You have tried hard,
been nice to people. –
maybe nicer than you should.
How long can this go on?

Until you don't care anymore.
Then in a desert breeze,
a written word, a flower's heart,
you hear the temple gong:

you already have it,
you've had it all along.

A Certain Age

Colors are the deeds and sufferings of light ~ Goethe

It has been said the weather is bright blue
this time of year. A tinge of cobalt cools
the contours, copper trembles, sounding true.
Red and golden maple leaves, the motley fools,
die dancing on a breeze of nevermore.
Those who must learn go back to schools.

The year was started long before
this current, nearer to the final, page
of curling calendar behind the closet door;
yet blood, air, the purple-kissed greengage
belie that paper rubric and bestir unnerving
promise in what's more than come of age.

Cliché favors youth, the tight uncurving
blade of spring, bronze beauty at the beach,
the summer's salad days all undeserving.
And youth favors cliché, believing each
grey hint of winter is a closing down,
smug in its grasp of things beyond its reach.

We've been there. Now we're here, my frown,
searching a spattered mirror for small clues
to an unsettling ripening. We grope for nouns
to name it – for the way so many hues
exquisitely become a potent reticence of brown.

Under the Dog Star

Under the dog star, weary, wilted,
watching dark's descent compress
all things to a lonesome distant barking
and a jittery sleeplessness –

I try TV for company
knowing I won't find it there
but needing noise and light
against the stupefying humid air –

ah, perfect! Verdi's Requiem
enters the room: air-stabbing bows
of violins, the maestro's frantic waves
and all the choral mouths agape with O's –

it is the final movement, the Libera Me:
"Deliver me from everlasting death…"
it screams, wails, rushes to a supreme hush
of sorrow's softening under the breath –

and in the silence afterward, deliverance
from dark, and grief. Hair of the dog, what
power this sad music has, to liberate
when other helps are absent and the need is great.

The Snow Will Make No Noise

The snow will make no noise, but clasp the ground in silence,
slowly muffling, snuffing-out, all but the sound of silence.

A blood moon will rise beyond the last wisps of withered
wheat
and deepening chills of wind blow circles around the silence.

Old uncle at the festivities, mostly a piece of history, still
he will hear a calliope, watch a merry-go-round in silence.

Sometimes the songs my mother never sang to me
drift on the blown flurries over her stony mound of silence.

So many poems have simply died for a lack of sounding;
are locked, like the terminal years of Ezra Pound, in silence.

What cannot be said, once and for all, howls dreadfully
like a two-headed dog that continues to hound the silence.

It was too early, earlier, and now it's become too late
to fix what broke or rewind the clocks unwound by silence.

See how kindness is kin to snow in the darkness –
flakes floating down to a stately, dumbfounded silence.

Delusion of Camels

They say another storm will come tonight
another layer of white
another weight of wet
clamped tight and cold over all hope
of softening bulbs or green tongues testing
toward springlight.

Out there, pale marmoreal camels rest
lie low in wait
legs lost to sight
hump after hump of patience ruminates
in silent readiness for its next burdening
this arctic night.

How much is needed to drive mad
the weary watcher of another and another
dreary iteration of
unwilling hibernation
dragging the caravan across this blank
expanse of desolation?

They say a single straw is all it takes
a final straw added to overbearing weight
in deserts of hot sand.
Tonight on frozen land
I watch the camels, hoping something breaks.
I want the final flake.

Autumn in the Sky

… gathering swallows twitter in the sky. ~ John Keats, To Autumn

Come autumn, gathering swallows twitter in the sky;
their song portends oncoming bitter from the sky.

Chickadees hop amid the rose hips till
in pursuit of blue they flitter toward the sky.

Lingering gladioli lean along the fence
aiming one last blossom-spitter at the sky.

Indian summer, you old scoundrel, heartbreak
mocker of the stars, you are a counterfeiter of the sky.

Earlier darkness doesn't faze the ever-blinking
radio red eye of the transmitter in the sky.

Electronics do not know this is the melancholy
season, though they sense a jitter in the sky.

It is the season when things die, return to haunt
in guises ravelled by cloud-knitters in the sky.

When I am old…am I already old?…then I
will head, shed all this earthly litter, for the sky.

O hold me tight tonight, you cold, you bright
immutable, you ever-fickle glitter in the sky.

North, Early December

Let me down easy

the way hints of winter
fall exquisitely today
scattering icy lacy flowers
from a cloud bouquet

flutter, waver just a bit
unhurried and unworried
to get on with it.

A deeper cold will come
but stay its harder hand
let play a little longer
the November grey indefinites

let me down easy.

The longest night is still ahead
weighs heavy in the apprehension
threatening dismay

let me go haltingly into its
frozen moonlit desolation
tempered by the touch of
something of its opposite

knowing I am anyway
to be let down, I pray

let me down easy.

Now is the Fall

Lenders continue to love their usurious way of falling
while grubbers hover above a penurious way of falling.

An ill wind blows at the lady's presumptive tiara;
how it cackles upon her perjurious way of falling.

"I laid me down with a will," R. L. Stevenson wrote;
Dylan Thomas raved a fume-furious way of falling.

A comedown is sometimes called a comeuppance but
my tuppence deems that a spurious way of falling.

A warning to those who topple off ladders: bracing
to save yourself is a most injurious way of falling.

When fish die, they turn upside-down and rise
in the water; this is their curious way of falling.

I dream I leap into heaped colors of new-fallen leaves
fingers crossed for a windup luxurious way of falling.

Night Draws Near, Brother Ass

Night draws near, brother ass;
pale sister moon ascends the dark,

brother wind makes a chill pass
from long ago and far away
where Francis dogs still bark –

they echo sorry old beliefs
that make you lesser than
a thing that's called a soul.

As if some merciless sneak thief
has stripped you of your rigmarole,

stolen all your oomph for dreams
of grasping the elusive carrot
and your fear of prodding stick,

you slow a bit now, and seem weary
though you stubbornly as ever climb
the slope of each day, brick by brick.

You've been a good and faithful
servant – more than I can say

for parts that think and speak.
Yours is an understanding deeper
than all hope and pray. Are we perhaps

at last in sempiternal unison about
the moment that must come? Then
let's together bray…and bray…and bray!

Addendum

Louise Labé (1524-1566)

A Celebration in Translation

L ouise Labé was born in Lyon, France, the daughter of a wealthy ropemaker and his second wife. She was educated in Greek, Latin, Italian and Spanish. She was also taught music, specifically the lute, and was a renowned horsewoman and archer. Labé wrote prose and poetry including three elegies and 24 sonnets.

Cynthia Jobin enjoyed translating Labé's sonnets with a free hand to express and celebrate the spirit of the originals. Three of her translations have been selected for inclusion here together with the 16th century French texts.

Sonnet VIII

I live, I die. I burn, I drown.
Enduring cold, I am most hot.
Life is too hard, and it's too soft.
Joy insinuates when I am down.

I can weep suddenly, or be a clown;
Know torment and take pleasure in the lot.
It flees, yet it endures, what wealth I've got.
I am a desert, yet in green abound.

So love takes me to and fro
That in my deepest misery
The pain is gone before I know.

And when I'm confident the glow of
Happiness will last forever at its apogee –
I am reduced again to my first woe.

Sonnet VIII

Je vis, je meurs: je me brule et me noye.
J'ay chaut estreme en endurant froidure:
La vie m'est et trop molle et drop dure.
J'ay grans ennuis entremeslez de joye:

Tout à un coup je ris et je larmoye,
Et en plaisir maint grief tourment j'endure:
Mon bien s'en va, et à jamais il dure:
Tout en un coup je seiche et je verdoye.

Ainsi Amour inconstamment me meine:
Et quand je pense avoir plus de douleur,
Sans y penser je me treuve hors de peine.

Puis quand je croy ma joye estre certeine,
Et estre au haut de mon désiré heur,
Il me remet en mon premier malheur.

Sonnet IX

As soon as I begin to drift anew
In my bed's feathery soft cave,
Toward the restfulness I crave,
Sadness wanders off, dissolves in you.

Then I realize the good that I pursue
And sigh so loudly for, I hold engraved
In my own heart, and I am laved
With such fierce sobbing I could break in two.

O happy night all mine! O gentle drowse,
Sweet rest so filled with peace –
Carry on my dream as nights go by.

And if my loving soul is not supposed
Ever to have good things in truth, at least
Then, let me have them in a lie.

Sonnet IX

Tout aussi tôt que je commence à prendre
Dens le mol lit le repos désiré,
Mon triste esprit hors de moy retiré
S'en va vers toy incontinent se rendre.

Lors m'est avis que dedens mon sein tendre
Je tiens le bien, où j'ay tant aspiré,
Et pour lequel j'ay si haut souspiré,
Que de sanglots ay souvent cuidé fendre.

O dous sommeil, o nuit à moy heureuse!
Plaisant repos, plein de tranquilité,
Continuez toutes les nuiz mon songe:

Et si jamais ma povre âme amoureuse
Ne doit avoir de bien en vérité,
Faites au moins qu'elle en ait en mensonge.

Sonnet XII

Lute, dear companion of my discontent,
Innocent witness to my sighs,
Fair steward of my sad outcries,
How often you have joined in my lament.

So bothered by my mood's descent
That having once begun to improvise
A happy tune you suddenly revise it,
Mimicking my plaintive instrument.

And should I bid you play a major key
You hold back, in the minor, silence me –
Seeing how I sigh so tenderly again

You give expression to my tale of woe
And I am held back from self-pity in the hope
Your sadness brings my sadness to an end.

Sonnet XII

Lut, compagnon de ma calamité,
De mes soupires témoin irreprochablle,
De mes ennuis controlleur veritable,
Tu as souvent avec moy lamenté:

Et tant le pleur piteus t'a molesté,
Que commençant quelque son delectable,
Tu le rendois tout soudein lamentable,
Feignant le ton que plein avait chanté.

Et si te veus efforcer au contraire,
Tu te destens et si me contreins taire:
Mais me voyant tendrement soupirer,

Donnant faveur à ma tant triste pleinte:
En mes ennuis me plaire suis contreinte,
Et d'un dous mal douce fin esperer.

Notes

Anumber of these poems appeared previously in *A Certain Age*, published privately as a limited edition by Cynthia Jobin.

The following poems were published in *Indra's Net*, an international anthology of poetry published by Bennison Books:

The Sun Also Sets
Ode to a Condiment
Getting It

Notes on individual poems

Into Something Rich and Strange

Full fathom five thy father lies;
Of his bones are coral made;
Those are pearls that were his eyes:
Nothing of him that doth fade
But doth suffer a sea-change
Into something rich and strange.

(From Shakespeare's *The Tempest*, part of 'Ariel's song', Act one, scene two)

Crepuscule

This poem is written in the demanding Irish poetic form Séadna.

Unfallen Rain

Lately, I have been attempting poems in the Arabic form known as the ghazal (pronounced 'ghuzzle'). I have avoided it in the past because, like haiku, it has been widely misunderstood by a popular rush to adapt it to English and fallen far from the mark in both letter and spirit.

But I've been reading the poet Agha Shahid Ali (1949-2001) who clearly explains the requirements and promulgates good examples of the ghazal in English. He's convinced me of the possible power of the form, classically rendered, in the English language, and I am enjoying working with it as much as – though quite differently from – the sonnet. ~ Cynthia Jobin

Sung Exhortation to my Heart, in the Shower

It wasn't Orpheus's season in hell that did him in. It was that he turned to look back. ~ Cynthia Jobin

Poetry These Days

With apologies to my friend, Marta Nussbaum Steele, who once presented a poem by this title on the dissecting table of a poetry workshop in Harvard Square.

I had been reading T.S. Eliot's The Use of Poetry and The Use of Criticism and was enjoying a classic double martini when these lines occurred in the space of ten minutes. ~ Cynthia Jobin

A Fib

Of late, the inventors of poetry forms have caught on to a gimmick, now floating among the arts, of using the Fibonacci Sequence as a model for composition. It's a mathematical sequence of numbers in which each number is derived by adding the previous two numbers.

The poets who like to count syllables have adapted it so that each line of a poem is to follow the sequence by its number of syllables. They call it a 'Fib'. This is the first one I have ever written, and likely the last. ~ Cynthia Jobin

Sleep My Little Cabbage

'Fais do-do' is a French expression, 'do-do' being a diminutive of the verb 'dormir' (to sleep). It is a way of saying go to sleep, usually to small children. 'Mon p'tit chou' is literally 'my little cabbage' but is used figuratively as an affectionate expression like the English 'my pet'. ~ Cynthia Jobin

Palimpsest

'Laborare et orare' means 'to work is to pray'. This is a precept of the Benedictine Order.

Chrysoprase is an apple-green gemstone. It is associated with strengthening the workings of insight and the higher consciousness.

A Great Reckoning in a Little Room

Christopher Marlowe died after being stabbed in the eye in a brawl over who should pay for food and drink in an inn at Deptford, London, on 30 May 1593. Shakespeare referred to this in *As You Like It* as 'a great reckoning in a little room'.

Touchstone is the jester in Shakespeare's *As You Like It*.

Griselda

I began with the Germanic source of the name, i.e. 'gris hild' meaning 'dark battle' after reading the life of Eleanor Roosevelt and her battle with depression – a mood spirit she called 'Griselda'.

Griselda is somewhat like that downer Winston Churchill called his 'black dog', which I'm sure we all know at one time or another. ~ Cynthia Jobin

February Fill-Dyke

The saying 'February fill-dyke, be it black or white' is a reference to rain (black) or melting snow (white) filling dykes with water in the often rainy month of February.

Tefnut is a goddess of moisture, moist air, dew and rain in Ancient Egyptian religion.

MaryMartha

In the Bible, Luke 10, verse 40, two sisters, Mary and Martha, welcome Jesus into their house. Martha, busy serving, complains to Jesus about Mary sitting at his feet to listen to his teaching.

Should the Ability Appear

"…I love the idea of sitting in the sun reading, and often go out with my book—but the pages remain unread as I sit and muse and look and dream—but the book is there should the ability to read outside suddenly appear" ~ a comment on Cynthia Jobin's blog that inspired her to write this poem.

Walking on Water

A loon is a North American aquatic bird; an alewife is a north-western Atlantic fish that swims up rivers to spawn.

January

The Roman god Janus is the guardian of doorways and gates, usually represented with two faces so he can look both backwards and forwards.

Fiddleheads

Fiddlehead is a North American name for young, curled edible fern fronds.

In the Shallows

This poem is written in the demanding Irish poetic form Séadna.

Night Draws Near, Brother Ass

Saint Francis of Assisi (1181-1226) referred to his own body as 'Brother Ass', punishing it when, for example, sorely tempted. However, before he died he asked his body to be pardoned for having treated it with such cruelty.

This poem draws on Saint Francis of Assisi's 'Canticle of the Sun' (also know as 'Laudes Creaturarum' – 'Praise of the Creatures'.) composed while he was recovering from an illness. In it, Saint Francis celebrates 'Brother Sun', 'Sister Moon', 'Brother Wind', 'Sister Water', 'Brother Fire' and 'Mother Earth'. He also refers to 'our Sister Bodily Death' from whom no one can escape.

'Francis dogs' is written without a possessive apostrophe in this poem. The editors discussed whether Cynthia may have meant to add one (Francis' dogs) but, on balance, decided to leave this line as she had written it.

The poem was completed shortly before her death.

Bennison Books

Bennison Books has four imprints:

Contemporary Classics
Great writing from new authors

Non-Fiction
Interesting and useful works written by experts

People's Classics
Handpicked golden oldies by favourite and forgotten authors

Poetic Licence
Poetry and prosetry

Bennison Books is named after Ronald Bennison,
an aptly named blessing.

Bennisonbooks.com

www.ingramcontent.com/pod-product-compliance
Lightning Source LLC
Chambersburg PA
CBHW061720020426
42331CB00006B/1017